CELLO

PATRIOTIC FAVORITES

Solos and String Orchestra Arrangements
Correlated with Essential Elements String Method

Arranged by
JOHN MOSS

T0053198

Welcome to Essential Elements Patriotic Favorites! There are two versions o. .... versatile book. The SOLO version appears in the beginning of your book. The STRING ORCHESTRA arrangements of each song follows. The supplemental CD recording or string orchestra PIANO PART may be used as an accompaniment for solo performance. Use these recordings when playing solos for friends and family.

ISBN 0-634-05281-0

HAL•LEONARD®
CORPORATION
7777 W. BLUEMOUND RD. P.O. BOX 13819 MILWAUKEE, WI 53213

00868066

GOD BLESS AMERICA®

CELLO
Solo

Words and Music by
IRVING BERLIN
Arranged by JOHN MOSS

YANKEE DOODLE

CELLO
Solo

Traditional
Arranged by JOHN MOSS

THE CAISSONS GO ROLLING ALONG/ANCHORS AWEIGH

CELLO
Solo

Arranged by JOHN MOSS

MY COUNTRY, 'TIS OF THEE (AMERICA)/
AMERICA, THE BEAUTIFUL

CELLO
Solo

Arranged by JOHN MOSS

From the Motion Picture THE PATRIOT

THE PATRIOT

CELLO
Solo

Composed by JOHN WILLIAMS
Arranged by JOHN MOSS

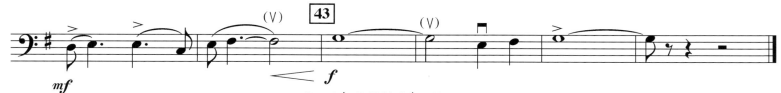

00868066

MARINE'S HYMN

CELLO
Solo

Words by HENRY C. DAVIS
Melody based on a theme by
JACQUES OFFENBACH
Arranged by JOHN MOSS

STARS AND STRIPES FOREVER

CELLO
Solo

By JOHN PHILIP SOUSA
Arranged by JOHN MOSS

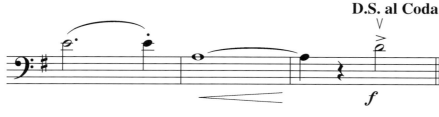

00868066

BATTLE HYMN OF THE REPUBLIC

CELLO
Solo

Words by JULIA WARD HOWE
Music by WILLIAM STEFFE
Arranged by JOHN MOSS

THIS IS MY COUNTRY

CELLO
Solo

Words by DON RAYE
Music by AL JACOBS
Arranged by JOHN MOSS

THE STAR SPANGLED BANNER

CELLO
Solo

Words by FRANCIS SCOTT KEY
Music by JOHN STAFFORD SMITH
Arranged by JOHN MOSS

From the Paramount and DreamWorks Motion Picture SAVING PRIVATE RYAN

HYMN TO THE FALLEN

CELLO
Solo

JOHN WILLIAMS
Arranged by JOHN MOSS

GOD BLESS AMERICA®

CELLO
String Orchestra Arrangement

Words and Music by
IRVING BERLIN
Arranged by JOHN MOSS

YANKEE DOODLE

CELLO
String Orchestra Arrangement

Traditional
Arranged by JOHN MOSS

With Spirit

00868066

THE CAISSONS GO ROLLING ALONG/
ANCHORS AWEIGH

CELLO
String Orchestra Arrangement

Arranged by JOHN MOSS

00868066

MY COUNTRY, 'TIS OF THEE (AMERICA)/ AMERICA, THE BEAUTIFUL

CELLO
String Orchestra Arrangement

Arranged by JOHN MOSS

MY COUNTRY, 'TIS OF THEE (AMERICA)
Words by SAMUEL FRANCIS SMITH
Music from THESAURUS MUSICUS
Copyright © 2003 by HAL LEONARD CORPORATION
International Copyright Secured   All Rights Reserved

AMERICA, THE BEAUTIFUL
Words by KATHERINE LEE BATES
Music by SAMUEL A. WARD
Copyright © 2003 by HAL LEONARD CORPORATION
International Copyright Secured   All Rights Reserved

From the Motion Picture THE PATRIOT

THE PATRIOT

CELLO
String Orchestra Arrangement

Composed by JOHN WILLIAMS
Arranged by JOHN MOSS

Colonial March

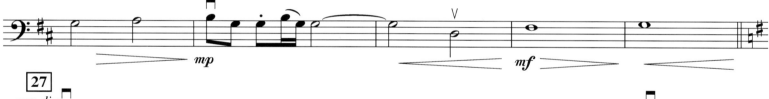

MARINE'S HYMN

CELLO
String Orchestra Arrangement

Words by HENRY C. DAVIS
Melody based on a theme by
JACQUES OFFENBACH
Arranged by JOHN MOSS

March style

STARS AND STRIPES FOREVER

CELLO
String Orchestra Arrangement

By JOHN PHILIP SOUSA
Arranged by JOHN MOSS

00868066

BATTLE HYMN OF THE REPUBLIC

CELLO
String Orchestra Arrangement

Words by JULIA WARD HOWE
Music by WILLIAM STEFFE
Arranged by JOHN MOSS

THIS IS MY COUNTRY

CELLO
String Orchestra Arrangement

Words by DON RAYE
Music by AL JACOBS
Arranged by JOHN MOSS

THE STAR SPANGLED BANNER

Words by FRANCIS SCOTT KEY
Music by JOHN STAFFORD SMITH
Arranged by JOHN MOSS

CELLO
String Orchestra Arrangement

From the Paramount and DreamWorks Motion Picture SAVING PRIVATE RYAN

HYMN TO THE FALLEN

CELLO
String Orchestra Arrangement

JOHN WILLIAMS
Arranged by JOHN MOSS

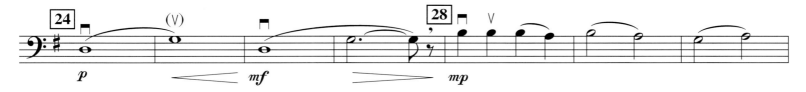

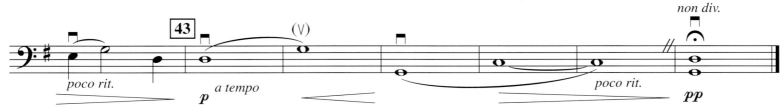

00868066

MORE FAVORITES FROM ESSENTIAL ELEMENTS

These superb collections feature favorite songs that students can play as they progress through their string method books. Each song is arranged to be played by either an orchestra or by soloists, with optional accompaniment on CD.

Each song appears twice in the book, featuring:
- Solo instrument version
- String arrangement for orchestra or ensembles
- Accompaniment CD included with conductor's score
- Accompaniment CD available separately
- Piano accompaniment book that is compatible with recorded backgrounds

Available:
- Conductor
- Violin
- Viola
- Cello
- String Bass

- Accompaniment CDs
- Value Starter Pak
  (includes 24 Student books
  plus Conductor Book w/CD

CHRISTMAS FAVORITES
Arranged by Lloyd Conley
Songs include:
The Christmas Song
  (Chestnuts Roasting
  on an Open Fire)
Frosty the Snow Man
A Holly Jolly Christmas
Jingle-Bell Rock
Let It Snow! Let It Snow! Let It Snow!
Rockin' Around the Christmas Tree
We Wish You a Merry Christmas

BROADWAY FAVORITES
Arranged by Lloyd Conley
Songs include:
Beauty and the Beast
Cabaret
Edelweiss
Get Me to the Church on Time
I Dreamed a Dream
Go Go Go Joseph
Memory
The Phantom of the Opera
Seventy Six Trombones

MOVIE FAVORITES
Arranged by Elliot Del Borgo
Includes themes from:
An American Tail
Chariots of Fire
Apollo 13
E.T.
Forrest Gump
Dances with Wolves
Jurassic Park
The Man from Snowy River
Star Trek
Mission: Impossible

PATRIOTIC FAVORITES
Arranged by John Moss
Songs include:
America, the Beautiful
Battle Hymn of the Republic
God Bless America
Hymn to the Fallen
My Country, 'Tis of Thee (America)
The Patriot
The Star Spangled Banner
Stars and Stripes Forever
This Is My Country
Yankee Doodle

FOR MORE INFORMATION, SEE YOUR LOCAL MUSIC DEALER,
OR WRITE TO:

HAL•LEONARD®
CORPORATION
7777 W. BLUEMOUND RD. P.O. BOX 13819 MILWAUKEE, WI 53213
Visit Hal Leonard Online at **www.halleonard.com**

Prices, contents, and availability subject to change without notice.
Some products may not be available outside the U.S.A.

0210